MW01625767

ANIMAL LIVES

The Barn Owl

KINGFISHER
Kingfisher Publications Plc
New Penderel House, 283–288 High Holborn,
London WC1V 7HZ

First published by Kingfisher Publications Plc 1999
ISBN 0 7534 0315 3

This edition published in 1999 for
The Book People Ltd, Hall Wood Avenue,
Haydock, St Helens WA11 9UL
ISBN 1 85613 527 6

1BP / 0499 / SC / RPR(NEW) / 150NYM

A CIP catalogue record for this book is available from the British Library.

Editor: Christian Lewis
Series editor: Miranda Smith
Series designer: Sarah Goodwin

Printed in Hong Kong / China

ANIMAL LIVES

The Barn Owl

Illustrated by
Bert Kitchen

Written by
Sally Tagholm

TED SMART

The barn owl sits motionless on the gate, a ghostly shape in the slowly gathering dusk. The winter fields are frozen, the trees bare and the landscape deserted. Small creatures, such as long-tailed field mice, do not stray far from home. With food so hard to find, the owl will have to leave his favourite patch tonight. The pale sun has almost disappeared from view. It is time to hunt.

He swoops slowly over the trees and hedges, across the rolling countryside, leaving the gate far behind. A silent phantom, his huge wings quietly beat the night air, their soft downy surface deadening the sound. Under the splendid feathers, his body is slim and surprisingly light – a perfect flying machine. With his super-efficient sense of hearing, and big, round eyes that can see in the dark, he will find a plump mouse or juicy rat before long. He might even come across a flock of small birds roosting in some frosty hedgerow.

The barn owl slows down and almost comes to a halt. He has found what he is looking for. He hovers, suspended in the dark night air. Eyes fixed on a small brown mouse perched on the trunk of a fallen tree, he bides his time. Suddenly he plunges, snatching his prey, folding it in the vice-like grip of his deadly claws. He flies off triumphantly, his prize hanging from his beak.

Spring is here, the trees are in bud, and small creatures scurry and scratch after the long, cold winter. After months of roosting alone, the barn owl has found a mate. From his perch on the gate his blood-curdling screech pierces the still night air. The female answers and they twist and turn in the air, calling to each other and playing catch in the dark, like ghostly acrobats.

Now there is plenty of food in the hedgerows and ditches, the owl does not have to fly far to find a tasty long-tailed field mouse. He presents it to the female, a juicy offering which she swallows whole. Then he is off again in search of other food – the more the better. The female encourages him, begging for food by making special husky hisses that sound a bit like snoring. Sometimes, the male hovers in front of her in mid-air, fluttering his powerful wings. After she has fully accepted him, it will be time to mate.

The two owls roost together in the crumbling buildings of the deserted farm. The old haybarn is one of their favourite spots. It has a special owl window high up under the gable, which was built long ago when farmers wanted owls to help them wage war on rats and mice. Inside it is peaceful and dark up in the rafters – the perfect place to nest. The birds preen each other in the shadows.

After mating, the female lays a clutch of five smooth, white eggs, one at a time. This happens over ten days and she warms them by sitting tight on her nest high in the rafters above a few forgotten bales of straw and some rusty farm machinery. She only goes off duty to preen and stretch her wings outside. At regular intervals, she stands up and turns the eggs to make sure that they are heated evenly, pushing them around with her face and bill. They soon get a bit dirty because the nest is really just a layer of dry old owl pellets – the scattered fur, feathers and tiny bones of undigested prey. The remains of several small rodents, brought in by the male to feed his mate weeks ago, lie rotting in the straw nearby.

The barn owl is busy hunting the fields and hedgerows, bringing back whatever he can find to his hungry mate. This time it is a short-tailed vole – the barn owl's favourite food. The days go slowly by and she sits patiently on the eggs, hardly moving. After four long weeks, the brooding female becomes restless. At last, she can hear faint, cheeping calls from inside her first egg.

Tiny cracks appear on the shell as the first chick gets ready to leave his safe, warm world. He has a special bump on top of his beak – an egg tooth – to help him push his way out. Blind and helpless, his scrawny pink body unfolds like a tiny dinosaur. Two days later, a second egg hatches. The mother feeds her new chicks with scraps torn from freshly delivered prey. By the time the last egg hatches, the first chick is ten days old and his eyes are about to open.

With so many mouths to feed, the male hunts before dusk and after dawn, as well as at night. He brings in the odd frog or little bird, and a constant supply of small mammals. The chicks' bodies are soon covered with fluffy white down, and their newly-opened eyes are black and beady. As they grow, their mother too spreads her wings, leaving the nest to hunt.

As their beautiful speckled grown-up feathers appear, the five owlets slowly lose their baby white fluff. They explore the nest, hopping around over the squashed pellets, their heads bobbing from side to side as they investigate in the gloom. Fearless, they soon search out every nook and cranny of the hayloft and peer through the old round window at the world outside. By now, the mother roosts away from the barn, coming back only to deliver fresh supplies. One by one, the young owls start to exercise their brand new wings. They experiment, stretching and flapping, preparing for their first, perilous flights. After almost two months, the first-hatched flies from the nest. His brothers and sisters soon follow.

It has been a long, hot summer and the farmers have finished bringing in the corn. The earth is baked hard and dusty under a sea of stubble. The fields are full of small, scuttling creatures that are easy targets for a pair of sharp claws. All five owlets are safely fledged. The barn owl and his mate, who only have themselves to feed now, sit quietly on the gate under a clear, moonlit sky.

THE BARN OWL

Scientific name: *Tyto alba.*

Nicknames: Screech owl, scritch owl, screaming owl, white owl.

Size: Male and female birds are about the same size, measuring about 33–35 centimetres from head to tail. Wingspan is about 85 centimetres.

Weight: Males usually weigh about 330 grams. Females weigh about 400 grams in the breeding season and 360 grams in winter.

Distribution: Worldwide. Barn owls are found in every continent except the polar regions, although they avoid mountainous regions, cold areas, very hot desert regions, and dense tropical forests.

Habitat: Open or lightly wooded countryside and farmland. Also grasslands, wetlands and plantations such as oil-palm, dates and conifer.

Prey: Small mammals, particularly voles, as well as rats, shrews, mice, frogs and small birds.

Nests: Deserted buildings, haybarns, church towers, holes in trees.

Eggs: Laid in early or late spring, depending on food supply. Second clutches are sometimes laid in summer. Minimum number of eggs: 2. Maximum number of eggs: 9. The eggs take about 31 days to hatch.

Near relatives: The grass owl (southern Africa), the sooty owl (New Guinea and Australia), and the masked owl (Indonesia and Australia).

BARN OWLS IN THE COUNTRYSIDE

Barn owls normally keep well out of sight, flying by night and roosting in quiet, undisturbed places during the day. However, it is sometimes possible to see one hunting on a wintry day, or carrying prey back to its young at dusk or dawn in midsummer. You may even catch a glimpse of a barn owl in the car headlights at night. Watch out for shiny black pellets or pale moulted feathers in old deserted farm buildings, but never approach or disturb the birds, particularly when they are nesting.

CONSERVATION

Although it was found all over Europe in the past, the barn owl is now a rare and endangered bird. Its numbers have declined dramatically this century as farmers have cleared land to make gigantic fields to produce more and more food such as cereal crops. The barn owl's natural hunting-grounds are vanishing as hedges, ditches and rough grasslands disappear. Their nesting sites are in danger too, as hollow trees are cut down and old buildings demolished or converted. Barn owl conservation groups have begun to take action, preserving the rough grasslands, which are rich in prey. They also provide nest boxes.

BARN OWL WORDS

bill a bird's beak
brooding sitting on eggs to keep them warm and hatch them out
clutch a group of eggs laid at one time
down a bird's soft baby feathers
egg tooth the bump on the top of a baby owl's beak that it uses to break out of its shell during hatching
fledged fully feathered and able to fly
mammal an animal that produces milk to suckle its young
pellet dried mass of undigested food such as bones and fur
preen to trim and clean feathers with the beak
prey animal or bird that is hunted for food
rodent animal such as a rat or mouse that is hunted as prey by the barn owl
roost perching or resting place
screech the barn owl's harsh scream

USEFUL CONTACTS

The Barn Owl Trust
Waterleat, Ashburton,
Devon TQ13 7HU
Tel: 01364 653026

Young Ornithologists' Club (YOC)
Royal Society for the Protection of Birds (RSPB),
The Lodge, Sandy,
Bedfordshire SG19 2DL
Tel: 01767 680551

Wildlife Watch,
The Green, Waterside South,
Lincoln LN5 7JR
Tel: 01522 544400

Bird Life International,
Wellbrook Court,
Girton Road,
Cambridge CB3 0NA
Tel: 01223 277318

INDEX

ACKNOWLEDGEMENTS

The author and publishers are grateful for the help and advice that David Ramsden of the Barn Owl Trust has given them in the preparation of this book, and thank Muriel Kitchen and Mike Davis for the photographs on the jacket.